Profitable Child Care
How to Generate More Income for Your Child Care Business

Lisa Pennington

Although the author has made every effort to ensure that the information in this book was correct at press time, the author does not assume the information is correct at present and hereby disclaims any liability to any party for any loss, damage, or disruption caused by errors or omissions, whether such errors or omissions result from negligence, accident, or any other cause.
Copyright © 2015 by Lisa Pennington
Cover Design by Martin Hammond
Formatting and Production by Denise McGrail
Editing by Denise McGrail
ISBN: 978-1511806169
eBook ISBN: 978-0-9910936-4-9
All rights reserved.
No part of this book may be reproduced, scanned or distributed in any printed or electronic form without permission. Please do not participate or encourage piracy of copyrighted materials in violation of the author's rights.
First published in the United States in 2015
For inquiries, please contact the author directly at:
www.startmychildcarebusiness.com
penni2012@hotmail.com

DEDICATION

To my family for their unwavering support for all my adventures!

CONTENTS

Foreword   1

Chapter 1 - Structure Your Business to Be Profitable   5
    Introduction
    Legal Benefits of Registering as an LLC
    Tax Benefits of Registering as an LLC
    Registering as an LLC
    Common LLC Misconceptions
    Key Points from Chapter 1

Chapter 2 - Create a Map for Your Child Care Center's Financial Future   23
    Introduction
    Benefits of a Business Plan
    Executive Summary
    The Demand Statement
    Proposed Business Concept
    Capital Requirements
    Financial Projections
    The Risk Statement
    Competition
    Founder and Contact Information
    Hiring a Business Plan Writer
    Key Point from Chapter 2

Chapter 3 - Increase Your Child Care Center's Wealth as a Non-Profit Organization   45
    Introduction
    The Nuts and Bolts of 501(c)(3) Status
    Charitable Donations
    How to Find and Apply for Grants
    Grant Resources
    Grant Writing Scams

Key Points from Chapter 3

Chapter 4 - Train for Success   65
    Introduction
    Train the Trainer
    Management Credentials
    Staffing Concerns
    Key Points from Chapter 4

Chapter 5 - Profitable Management Strategies   89
    Introduction
    How to Deal with Low Enrollment
    How to Handle Parent Complaints and Safeguard Your Center's Reputation
    How to Deal with Competing Child Care Centers
    How to Address Fiscal Management Concerns
    Key Points from Chapter 5

Conclusion   102

About the Author   104

Resources   105

FOREWORD

With more and more parents working outside of the home the demand for child care is on the rise. According to statistics provided by the Center for American Progress, only one-third of children are cared for by a full-time, stay-at-home parent. This translates into approximately 12 million children in the United States under the age of five that require quality child care. For small child care operations this means there is opportunity for growth and profit knocking on the front door.

Whether you are just starting out on your child care journey or you already operate a small home center with the goal of transitioning into a larger operation, structuring your business correctly and developing a solid business plan is the key to sustaining a child care business that is lucrative and profitable even during times of low enrollment and an uncertain economy. A career in the child care industry is rewarding and enriching on many different levels, but managing a successful business in this industry also presents many challenges such as defending one's personal liability, securing funding, retaining qualified staff members, and attracting new business that can threaten your center's profitability.

Money-making child care programs understand the legal and financial benefits of structuring their businesses as limited liability companies (LLCs). Lucrative child care programs know the importance of expertly training their workers to ensure families always receive the best care possible. Financially successful centers know that sometimes choosing to operate as a 501(c)(3) non-profit company opens doors to programs and subsidies that will provide access to grants and other funding sources that you may not have otherwise been able to attain. By choosing to read, *Profitable Child Care, How to Generate More Income for Your Child Care Business*, you are taking that first step towards wealth and prosperity that nearly all child care providers seek, but don't always attain.

No matter what kind of child care center you operate (home-based, a small child care center, a faith-based daycare, etc.), this book will give you concise, useable information that you can apply to your day-to-day operations to help you increase your profit margin.

This book isn't about theory. It is about getting down to the nitty-gritty and keeping it real. The suggestions given within these pages have been used by actual child care centers throughout the country with stellar results. Of course, your own results will depend on what you are willing to put into the management and development of your business. But, if you follow the recommendations and seek out the resources within this book, there is no doubt that you will find the path of success paved in gold.

Lisa Pennington

CHAPTER 1
<u>Structure Your Business to Be Profitable</u>
Protect Your Personal Assets

INTRODUCTION

How you choose to legally structure your business will have a direct impact on your ability to profit and succeed in your business ventures. Too many child care providers take a casual approach to organizing their businesses. These individuals treat their child care operations as a hobby rather than a serious business endeavor; however, taking this approach can come back to bite you where it hurts most in respect to your financial standing.

One of the biggest mistakes a child care provider can make is to operate as a sole proprietorship. While this is a popular business structure in this industry, it is not necessarily the best way to legally protect your personal assets or safeguard your business. Many child care providers choose this business structure because it facilitates ease of operation. Unlike other business structures, a sole proprietorship is basically unfettered by government restrictions. You still have to report your income to the Internal Revenue Service (IRS), but you don't have to report to board members, partners, etc. You are free to make operational and financial decisions without the approval of anyone else but you.

Sounds great, right? Well, what if I told you that this manner of structuring a child care center is one of the surest ways to lose your home, your personal savings, your children's college savings, and any other assets held in your name? Do I have your attention? The lure of sole proprietorship with no strings attached may sound freeing, but you're actually at the mercy of your families' compassion and understanding if there is an accident while a child is in your care. In a nutshell, you and your personal assets are 100% liable.

What if I told you there was another way; a way that you could still retain control of your child care business without putting your personal assets at risk? Do I have your attention now?

LEGAL BENEFITS OF REGISTERING AS AN LLC

It is a common misconception that only multi-million dollar businesses, owned by numerous people, operate as limited liability companies (LLCs). In reality, this business structure is the ideal choice for structuring your child care operation to make certain that your personal assets are protected should an accident happen while a child is in your care or your business acquires a number of debts and you need to seek federal financial relief in the form of bankruptcy to payback your creditors.

Registering your child care center as an LLC defines your business as a separate legal entity. This means that as long as you do not personally guarantee any loans or expenses using your name and social security number, you do not have any personal responsibility to repay them. This falls on the business' shoulders.

So how does the LLC protect you?

Great question! The LLC structure increases your legal protection should a lawsuit be filed against the child care center by a parent, a creditor, or any other entity. It safeguards your personal assets so that your home, your personal savings, your vehicles, and any other personal monies are not considered a means for repayment should your child care center lose a lawsuit.

Let's take a look at an example of how the LLC structure can protect your assets. The following example tells Karin's story and demonstrates how the LLC structure saved her personal savings when business creditors came knocking on her door. For privacy purposes all names have been changed.

When I started my child care business, Little Angel's Daycare, I operated as a sole proprietor. I enjoyed knowing I could run a business without having to hire a slew of lawyers and business people to help me manage the taxes and payroll. It was just me and two other neighborhood moms who ran Little Angel's, so this way of operating my business made sense to me. But, then I heard of another child care provider in the neighborhood who owned a small child care business in the area who was being sued by a family, accusing the center of feeding their 3-year-old son food he was allergic to and putting his life at risk. The woman's entire life savings was at risk of being absorbed by the lawsuit.

This is when I decided to restructure Little Angel's as an LLC. Thank goodness I did because three years after restructuring, the local economy in my small Illinois town, took a major hit. There were several major employers that shut their doors and laid off their workers. Overnight my child care center lost five children - half of my registered families. Without this income and unable to find children to take their place, I could no longer afford to run my business effectively. I could no longer afford to pay back the loans I had taken out in the business' name to add educational supplies to our mixed-use classroom.

It wasn't long before the creditors came calling and demanding their payments. They threatened to garnish my husband's wages from his job to pay these debts and to garnish our personal bank accounts. Thankfully, because I restructured Little Angel's Daycare as an LLC several years prior, my personal assets were protected. The business still owed these debts, but my business' creditors could not come after mine or my husband's personal assets.

TAX BENEFITS OF REGISTERING AS AN LLC

Aside from the legal benefits of the LLC business structure, child care providers can also take advantage of the simplified tax filing benefits that this set-up offers. For individual business owners, the LLC offers the ability to be taxed as a sole proprietorship by filing out the one-person LLC form. The IRS calls this "pass through income."

The term "pass through income" means that the individual business owner can elect to have all the income from their business pass through onto their personal tax returns without affecting the owner's personal liability.

This is done by filling out IRS form 8832 and selecting the "disregarded entity" classification. When you file this form, your business income and losses are not considered a separate entity for tax purposes and all income, expenses, and losses can be reported on your personal tax return.

What if I have a business partner? Can I still form an LLC and receive the "pass through income" benefits?

Yes! This is just another wonderful benefit of filing as an LLC. Many husband and wife teams have formed LLCs and are running successful child care operations using this structure. Even if you're partnering with another person that is not your husband or wife, you can still take advantage of the "pass-through" tax status benefits by filing IRS form 8832 and selecting the "partnership" option on the form. Both you and your partner will include this form with your individual tax returns and each, individually, report your own profits, losses, and other business expenses. The difference with the partnership option is that you will need to also file IRS form 1065, which provides the IRS with information about the total income of the child care operation.

Another tax benefit, according to the Small Business Administration (SBA), is simplified recordkeeping. LLCs have fewer reporting and bookkeeping requirements than corporations (although this business structure does require a bit more work than the sole proprietorship structure where you usually only need to file a fictitious name report with the Secretary of State's office). However, we already determined that the sole proprietorship structure also offers zero personal liability protection. Although filing as an LLC is marginally more complicated, most single owners or partnerships can usually get by with using standard forms that can be found on their state tax and revenue websites.

As with any business venture, it is always advisable to hire a practiced tax professional who will not only be able to help you fill out the necessary forms required of LLCs, but to counsel you on the many other ways that this legal structure can help you protect your assets. This could be a tax preparer, a tax attorney, or another tax professional who has experience working with LLC registered child care centers and organizations.

REGISTERING AS AN LLC

An LLC is not mandated by federal law, but is an entity that is created and governed by state statute. What does this mean for you? If you are interested in restructuring your child care operation as an LLC, you need to check with the taxing authority in your state to determine the specific regulations that apply in your situation. A wonderful resource that will help you understand how your state deals with single-member LLCs can be found at the following website: http://www.nolo.com/legal-encyclopedia/single-member-llcs.html.

Do I need a taxpayer identification number?

For federal reporting purposes, single-member LLCs can generally use social security numbers to file income tax returns and other reporting requirements in regards to tax income. This is because, as a single-member LLC, you are regarded as a disregarded entity. However, there are certain exceptions.

For example, do have a payroll? Does your child care center employ staff members either full or part-time? Whether you have two people who help you out on a part-time basis or you manage a larger operation with numerous staff members, you will be required to have an Employee Identification Number (EIN).

You may also be required to file for an EIN if you open a bank account. While a sole proprietor can open a bank account and accept payments made out to the company with a fictitious name report on file, an LLC may not be afforded these same liberties.

When you form an LLC, you will need to take certain steps to make sure everything is done according to state statute. Again – and this cannot be repeated enough – you need to check with your individual state for their exact requirements. The following steps are general steps as outlined by the SBA that will help you organize the process and make the transition from a sole proprietorship to an LLC seamless and as smooth as possible.

Choose a Business Name

When selecting a name, you must follow three rules:

1. You must choose a unique name that is not already being used by another registered LLC in your state. This is not a requirement when registering a fictitious name; therefore, it may be necessary to rename your business to achieve LLC status. Most states have online search tools to make this process easier and avoid the frustration of having your name rejected after you've gone through the trouble of filing.

2. The name must include the acronym, LLC

3. Your business name may not include words that are controlled by state regulations. For example, nearly all states restrict the use of the words "bank" or "insurance" as part of a company name.

File the Articles of Organization Document

This document sounds scary, but it is really quite easy to complete and gives credibility to your LLC. This document will include the following information:

- Business name
- Business address
- Name of members with a controlling interest

The majority of states require that this document be filed with the Secretary of State, but this isn't an across-the-board rule. You'll want to make sure to check with your individual state to find out exactly where this report should be filed. Other government offices that the Articles of Organization document may need to be filed with may include: the Department of Commerce and Consumer Affairs, Division of Corporations and Commerce, and/or the State Corporation Commission.

A filing fee may also be required.

Produce an Operating Agreement

This document is not required in most states when operating as a single-member LLC or a two-member LLC. So, why would you want to create an operating agreement?

This agreement includes information about members' rights and responsibilities, the allocation of profits and losses, it details rules and regulations regarding the business, and strengthens the structure of your business. If you function as a multi-member LLC (with more than two owners), an operating agreement is highly beneficial to your child care business.

Obtain Permits and Licenses

When you designate your business as an LLC, you are required to obtain specific permits and licenses. These requirements vary by state, locality, and industry. The SBA has a helpful resource on their website entitled, *Obtain Business Licenses and Permits*. It provides an overview of the various federal and state permit and licensing requirements, and it also incorporates an interactive search-and-find tool to help you figure out the exact forms you need for your state. The website address for this invaluable research tool is listed in the resource section at the end of this book.

The SBA also has several resources for women-owned, small businesses. To learn more about the SBA Women-Owned Small Business Program, refer to the website information in the resource section at the end of the book.

Public Statements

The final step in forming an LLC is to formally announce your intent to operate under your chosen name in your selected locality. The practice of announcing one's business is not widely adopted by the majority of states, but there are still some states like New York and Arizona that require newly formed LLCs to publish information in a local newspaper about their formation.

Before you waste your money publishing in a newspaper, find out if your state requires publication. This information can be found by contacting your business filing office.

In addition to the SBA website, the IRS website offers a number of articles related to the topic of single-member LLCs and two-member LLCs. Referencing the information on both the SBA's and IRS's websites in conjunction with speaking to a tax professional will help you determine the best way to set up your newly formed LLC child care business. And, as mentioned previously, depending on the state in which you live there may be additional requirements that you need to be aware of to file as an LLC in your state. This is why a tax professional is an invaluable collaborator to have on your team.

COMMON LLC MISCONCEPTIONS

While the LLC structure does provide tremendous personal asset protection, child care providers of small, mid-sized, and large operations still need to understand the limitations of the LLC umbrella of protection.

Bookkeeping

As an LLC, you are responsible for keeping clear and concise records. Although you do not need to report to board members or shareholders, accurate bookkeeping is essential. Any corporate protection an LLC gives you can essentially become null and void during a lawsuit if your financial records are a mess. Keep in mind that accurate bookkeeping is not only important from a legal standpoint, but it also makes applying for grants, loans, and other programs easier when everything is organized in an efficient and up-to-date manner.

Bookkeeping is also important if you ever decide to sell your business. Being able to show how much revenue your business generates on a monthly, quarterly, and yearly basis will help you prove the worth of your business.

Not every child care center owner is a proficient bookkeeper. Let's be honest. Many people get into this business because they want to provide a service and meet a need for the families in their local communities. They are not accountants. Furthermore, child care providers wear many hats throughout the day and sometimes trying to manage all aspects of a center's operation can become rather exhausting. It is no wonder that mistakes are made and bookkeeping is put off for another day.

Unfortunately, making a mistake in this business can cost you a good deal of money. This is why, if you're not committed to keeping precise financial records, you should hire someone who has this background and loves to work with numbers to manage this aspect of your business. If your budget doesn't have room to hire another person, consider investing in bookkeeping software specifically for child care providers.

Child care-specific bookkeeping software can help you do the following:

- Track family and agency balances
- Record payments
- Print family statements and receipts
- Develop account activity reports
- Manage accounts receivable
- Track bank deposit reports
- Print revenue and income reports

- Generate year-end tax statements
- Facilitate billing for divorced families
- Simplify billing for subsidized families
- General financial histories for families
- Complete center audits
- And more!

Bookkeeping software services make it easy to run your business and always know exactly where you are from a financial perspective. An example of inexpensive, easy to use bookkeeping software that you may want to consider is one called Minute Menu. Not only does this bookkeeping software help you keep track of billing and expenses, but it also offer valuable menu planning tools and features to make all aspect of child care management easy as 1-2-3.

If you prefer a more traditional bookkeeping kind of software, you may want to consider inexpensive payroll services such as Intuit QuickBooks for small businesses.

Professional Business Liability Insurance

As a child care provider, you have a legal responsibility to provide reasonable safekeeping to children while they are in your care. When either you or another member of your staff fails to meet these standards and a child is injured, falls ill, or is otherwise harmed, you can be held personally responsible. The law considers this an act of negligence and a breach of the duty of care. In situations like this, your LLC umbrella will not protect you. You and any other employee that is personally named in a lawsuit can be sued.

Professional business liability insurance, often called errors and omission insurance, gives your child care center the broadest personal liability coverage possible. This is a type of malpractice insurance that is often associated with doctors and lawyers, but gives you, the child care provider, an added layer of protection should accusations of neglect or abuse be brought against you in a civil lawsuit.

Purchasing professional business liability insurance is a must if you want to operate a successful and profitable child care business, and, in some states, this insurance coverage is mandatory. The truth is that no matter how safe and well-managed your child care operation is there is always a chance that something could happen that puts you in a precarious position.

Why risk your personal wealth?

Recommended personal business liability amounts are at least $1 million per occurrence and $2 million aggregate. Depending on the size of your child care business these amounts may vary. It is important to speak frankly with your insurance provider and consider personal business liability insurance an investment in your future and not merely another bill to pay or an expense you don't need. Every single child care provider needs this personal protection.

Before we move on to talking about the importance of developing a strong business plan for economic success, let me leave you with one final thought...

When you safeguard your business by forming an LLC, keeping accurate financial records, and going the extra mile to ensure that you're personal liability is defended, you are building a solid and secure business that is not at risk of financial failure.

If you do not structure your business as an LLC, you risk the following:

- Your home
- Your personal savings
- Your car
- Your credit rating

Why take this risk when forming an LLC is simple and straightforward?

KEY POINTS FROM CHAPTER 1

Structuring your child care center as an LLC protects your personal assets from being absorbed should a lawsuit be filed against your center.

Sole proprietorship is a legal structure that affords little personal protection and is not advised when operating a child care business.

Hiring a tax professional to help you register as a single-member LLC or LLC partnership, and file your income taxes, will ensure that the IRS recognizes your business income as "pass through income."

Accurate bookkeeping is essential to upholding any LLC corporate protection granted by state statue.

All child care providers should purchase professional business liability with a minimum of $1 million per occurrence and $2 million aggregate. The LLC umbrella will not protect your personal assets if you are sued for acting negligently or breaching your duty of care.

CHAPTER 2
Create a Map for Your Child Care Center's Financial Future
Tips for Developing a Business Plan to Improve Profitability

Lisa Pennington

INTRODUCTION

Obviously, when you started your child care business one of your primary goals was to create a profitable business; a business that would be sustainable in times of economic uncertainty and low enrollment. There are many variables that can have a direct impact on the financial success of your business and no one can determine with one hundred percent certainty just how profitable their child care center will be. But that doesn't mean you can't take steps to safeguard your business' financial future. One of the surest ways to do this is to take the time to develop a concise, well-written, and professionally structured business plan.

Operating any business without direction is like driving a car blindfolded and relying simply on luck to get you where you're going. Successful businesses, both large and small, use their business plans to help them identify their competition, their strengths and weaknesses, and other factors that will have a direct effect on how well they can expect their business to profit. In essence, your center's business plan is your roadmap to the pot of gold at the end of the rainbow. A well-developed business plan will show you the clearest path to reach that pot of gold. It will point out potential roadblocks and guide you around these obstacles so you can reach your destination with as few losses as possible.

Have you been operating without direction for a while? That's okay. It's a common mistake among first-time business owners, and even seasoned entrepreneurs can get ahead of themselves sometimes. Many people jump headfirst into business without testing the water. If you're struggling to compete in your local market or you're finding it difficult to get financial backing from potential investors, agencies, or other financial organizations, stop treading water and take a moment to develop a business plan. Not only will a business plan help you qualify for more substantial funding opportunities, it will also give you a better understanding of your business and make you a better businessperson.

As William Artzberger points out in his article entitled, *4 Steps to Creating a Stellar Business Plan*, your plan "serves to crystallize your business vision and guide you in fulfilling that vision." In this chapter, using examples from my own business plan for my child care business, Lisa's Little Ones, I'll show you why you need a business plan to help you achieve the level of financial success you desire.

BENEFITS OF A BUSINESS PLAN

We've already discussed the financial benefits of a business plan, but there are other advantages that you may not realize. A business plan points you in the right direction toward economic sustainability; however, it also gives you a deeper understanding of the nuts and bolts of not only your business, but of your industry. Business owners who do not have in-depth knowledge of the local child care industry and their target audience may struggle in terms of marketing, retention, and overall reception in the community.

Before we begin discussing the individual components of a well-structured business plan, take a quick look at the following ways that a business plan will benefit you:

- ➢ It outlines specific objectives for your child care center: It is a tool that evaluates and tracks how well your center is meeting its goals and what changes need to be made if those goals are not being adequately met.

- ➤ It recognizes your businesses strengths and weaknesses.
- ➤ It identifies your competition so programs or strategies can be put into place to effectively compete in the local market.
- ➤ It provides a realistic picture of what your profit and loss statements may look like by showing you what it will cost to operate your center and what steps must be taken in order to make a profit.
- ➤ It is a tool that can be used to apply for private and public funding.
- ➤ A good business plan adds value to your child care business. In the future, if you decide to sell, you will have solid evidence of what your business is worth to support your asking price.

Are you ready to start creating your business plan? Before we get started, please remember that the following examples are just an illustration of one particular type of business plan. Your plan may not look exactly like mine because there is not a one-size-fits-all model and your center may be structured differently, but you should try to include the following essential components as much as possible to make sure that your plan thoroughly addresses all points of concern:

- Executive Summary
- The Demand
- Proposed Business Concept
- Capital Requirements
- Projections
- Risk
- Competition

- Founder and Contact Information

EXECUTIVE SUMMARY

The executive summary is by far the most important part of your business plan. In this section you define what makes your child care center standout from the crowd, what your goals are for growth, and the exact steps you will take to make sure that your center succeeds. For business owners seeking investors or additional funding this is where first impressions are made. Whether you are a start-up or an established child care business revamping an original business plan, your executive summary should show that you understand the child care industry and that you've done your research. A well-written executive summary demonstrates that you have a clear understanding of what needs are not being met within your target audience and how your child care center can fill this void.

The following is an example of my executive summary that explains why a new daycare in an underserved population is important. As we go through the other sections of the business plan, you will most likely see a lot of this information repeated. That is okay. There will be parts of the plan that reiterate certain concepts. The goal of the executive summary is to touch on the major points that will be a part of your overall business plan.

Lisa's Little Ones – Executive Summary - Example

Quality child care is essential in communities where two-income families continue to grow and in the Texas communities of Farmersville, Melissa, Trenton, Leonard, Blue Ridge, McKinney, & Bonham, a severe daycare shortage remains. At present, with a population of over 65,000 families, the shortage of daycare options is serious.

With new road improvements and a new college campus being constructed, it is clear that the population in these cities will only continue to rise, while the daycare situation remains the same. The average commute to a child care center within these communities is 15 minutes. By establishing a center in the heart of these communities, we can dramatically reduce the commute for families seeking high quality daycare.

In our target area, the average family income is $56,000 with the average age of residents being 32 years old. Families are growing and these demographics clearly support that parents have the necessary income to pay for affordable and quality daycare.

Lisa's Little Ones will meet this demand with full care service from 6:30 a.m.-6:30 p.m. on weekdays. We will also offer occasional weekend services by appointment only. Our licensed and certified staff can serve the needs of 100 children on a daily basis in our 3,500 square foot facility that meets all safety requirement permits for children. Our services include meals, infant care, playtime, story time, physical education, and hands-on crafts.

We strive to be the best in the child care industry. Our experience and our desire to provide the highest quality child care will help us serve a dire need in the local community.

Obviously, your executive summary will be written in a manner that is tailored to your services, the needs in your community, and your overall business goals. However, every executive summary should contain the following:

- Mission statement
- Services offered
- Growth projections
- Company information
- Future plans

THE DEMAND STATEMENT

This is the part of your business plan where you will go into the specifics of why you need to expand your business or why you should start your business in the first place. Each child care center's demand statement will read differently depending on the gaps in their communities. For example, there may be an overwhelming number of child care centers in your community that provide daytime care, but you see a need for weekend and after-hours care. If this is the niche that your child care center is exploring, and you feel it could be a profitable venture, your demand statement should mention this lack of care in the community.

Another example may be that there are plenty of daycare centers that provide "babysitting," but very few quality preschool programs that focus early childhood education. Exploring the possibilities of offering this kind of child care service to families in your community could be quite profitable if you can demonstrate a need for those kinds of services.

In the following example, my demand statement demonstrates that there are a high percentage of two-income households in a cluster of several Texas communities. However, the nearest child care options are almost 15 minutes away. By identifying the need and supporting it with facts such as the average income and age of the families my center will serve, I am demonstrating that I will have children to serve and the families of my community can afford the child care services I am providing.

Lisa's Little Ones – The Demand Statement – Example

Quality child care is essential in communities where two income families continue to grow and in the Texas communities of Farmersville, Melissa, Trenton, Leonard, Blue Ridge, McKinney, & Bonham, a severe daycare shortage remains. With a population of over 65,000 families, the shortage of daycare remains a serious problem.

Average Distance to Proposed Day Care from all Towns: 15 minutes

Average Age: 32 years old

Average Income: $56,000

Examples of Continuous Growth:

- *New College*
- *Road Improvement of New Hwy*

PROPOSED BUSINESS CONCEPT

What do you hope to gain by starting a child care center or expanding the programs you currently offer? This section of the business plan helps you solidify your plans and organize your thoughts. Too many wonderful child care businesses fail because they do not have a solid business concept. Don't let this happen to you.

When developing your business concept, think about the demand in your community. Go back to the demand statement you wrote and think about what programs you can implement to meet these needs. For example, are you trying to meet the needs of families with special needs children in your community? Is this population of children underserved? If this is the gap your center plans to fill, then your business concept should specifically detail what programs will be put in place to assist these children. Will you be purchasing special learning tools or paying for staff trainings to help your staff better meet the needs of these children? Then your business should reflect these goals.

My business concept for Lisa's Little One's is written to reflect how my center will meet the needs of two-income, working families. It is short, simple, and to the point.

Lisa's Little Ones – Proposed Business Concept – Example

To create a quality daycare to meet the demand of two-income, working families with full care service from 6:30 a.m. - 6:30 p.m. weekdays and occasional weekend services by appoint only. Lisa's Little One's will serve 100 children daily in our 3,500 square foot facility. Our services will include the following:

- *Infant care*
- *Story time*
- *Play time*
- *Physical education*
- *Hands-on crafts*

All services will be provided by licensed and certified staff that has completed thorough background checks and drug testing.

Lisa's Little One's will host holiday events, gift making, and other activities that encourage families to take an active role in their children's care.

CAPITAL REQUIREMENTS

Anticipating financial need is how you build a successful and profitable child care business. If you'll be applying for funding, you'll need to show that you've done market research and know what the costs are to run your business. This knowledge allows you to set reasonable rates and know exactly how much money you need to bring in each month to avoid catastrophic financial losses.

This portion of your business plan is essentially an

overview of your operating budget. In this section, you'll list all of your expenses which include initial operating costs (if you're expanding or are a start-up), monthly lease payments, personnel payments, fees for permits, licensing, and staff training, food, and anything else you need to operate your business on a daily basis.

In the example provided below, you'll see that I don't have a long list of expenses; however, the expenses I do list are fairly significant. Your capital requirements may be different. Let's take a look at my capital requirements.

Lisa's Little Ones – Capital Requirements – Example

Initial Expenses

Land	*$30,000*
Facility/Modules	*$150,000*
Personnel	*$225,000*

Administration/Licensing/ Furnishings/Supplies/Fees
   $68,652

Total Initial
   $473,652

Monthly Expenses

Mortgage	*$4,000*
Personnel	*$21,303*

Phones/Supplies/Utilities   *$4,917*

Insurance/Fees/Maintenance
    $1,351

Food   *$6,800*

Outside Services   *$1,000*

<u>*State Fees*</u>   <u>*$100*</u>

Total Monthly
$39,471

Your capital requirements are not going to look like mine. How you determine your personal capital requirements depends on the nature of your center, your overall business goals, and your individual expenses. Below is a more inclusive list of items that you should consider when developing your own capital requirements:

- Rent/Mortgage
- Salaries of owner/manager
- Teacher salaries full-time
- Teacher salaries part-time
- Supplies
- Utilities
- Accounting software
- Liability insurance for staff and children
- Taxes, including Social Security
- Legal and other professional fees
- Conferences
- Trainings

- Advertising and promotions
- Maintenance
- Internet
- Loans payments
- Construction costs
- Equipment
- Licenses and permits
- Miscellaneous

Staying on top of your capital requirements will keep you in touch with your financial needs. After you've completed this part of your business plan, it is a good idea to revisit it once or twice a year. Make adjustments to your capital requirements as necessary to make sure you always know exactly how much money you need to operate your business so it stays profitable.

FINANCIAL PROJECTIONS

The only way to run a lucrative child care business is to know how much money is coming into the center at all times. Accounting and cash flow are two main requirements of any business plan. It is what funders and investors will analyze to make sure you have the means to support your financial requests. Here is an example of what your financial projections may look like:

Weekday Care Financial Projections

Monthly Tuition   *$47,797*

Government Reimbursement   *$6,500*

Total Monthly Income $54,297

Total Annual Income: $651,564

Lisa's Little One's will accommodate 100 full time children opening day.

This is a rather simplified financial overview; however, it clearly shows how much money the child care center is capable of pulling in when enrollment is at one hundred percent. When you compare your financial projections with your capital requirements, this is when the big picture starts to come into focus. It is at this point where you see how much wiggle room you have in your budget before you begin to cross the line from a profitable business to a struggling business.

If the numbers do not add up, you need to seriously consider what steps you can take to stay well above the red. Ask yourself the following questions:

- ➤ Can you increase enrollment?
- ➤ Do you need to raise rates?
- ➤ Do you need to let certain staff members go?
- ➤ Do you need to look for a cheaper facility?

These are tough questions to answer, but they're necessary when the numbers don't add up right.

Like your capital requirements, you need to update your financial projections on a quarterly, bi-annual, or annual basis depending on your individual situation. This is the only way you can make sure you're always making the wisest financial decisions to keep your business turning a profit.

THE RISK STATEMENT

While you have control over some aspects of your business, there are going to be circumstances that seem to arise out of the blue that can halt your operations faster than a blizzard in the Dallas-Fort Worth area. The key to surviving these complications is to anticipate risk. All businesses operate under a veil of risk. But, when you have a plan in place to respond to unfavorable situations, you'll be more likely to weather the storm and come out unscathed on the other side.

What risks could your child care center face? Here's a list of risks that I included in my business plan that were specific to Lisa's Little Ones when I started my business.

Risk #1: Unforeseen construction costs in the land configuration, such as parking, utilities, or modular conversion that may require additional work.

Risk #2: Low initial enrollment.

Risk #3: Availability of qualified staff

Risk #4: Financial earnings delayed

Once you've identified your risks, you'll want to reflect on how you can address these concerns should they come to pass. For example, with Risk #2, I put into action a pre-enrollment plan that included actively promoting my child care center before the doors ever opened. I did this several months in advance of the center's opening and also offered financial incentives to families who took advantage of my pre-enrollment program.

Your risks are going to look different than mine, but don't be fooled into thinking that there won't be any involved in starting or expanding your child care center. Also, reevaluate risk factors frequently so you always have a Plan B to keep your business turning a profit.

COMPETITION

What makes your business plan unique? The child care industry in many locations is overwhelmed with providers. What makes your child care center an exceptional place for parents to consider over all others in the neighborhood? Why should investors care about the success of your center?

In order to understand where you fit in in an oversaturated industry, you must be well aware of your competition. You need to know what they're doing well, what needs they are already successfully fulfilling, and what your competition is lacking. This will help you find your niche. Identifying your competition helps you recognize profitable business opportunities and gives you the chance to get in on the ground floor when establishing a new service.

Take a look at what I discovered about my competition when starting Lisa's Little Ones.

1. In Blue Ridge, the school opened an on-site daycare to care for teacher's children. This tells me that this may be a niche that is already being fulfilled and I might want to consider a different approach for a successful child care operation.

2. There is a quality daycare facility in Bonham, but it is at its capacity serving a community of 10,000. I can use this information to advertise to the families in this community that are not being served because they are on a waiting list.

So what does this information tell me? It tells me that while I may not be successful gaining full enrollment by marketing to Blue Ridge families, I can fill a need for Bonham families. This is the direction I should with my new daycare operation.

Identifying the needs of your community based on careful market analysis and research is essential to your success as a profitable child care business. When you underestimate your competition, you stunt your own growth.

FOUNDER AND CONTACT INFORMATION

Remember that your business plan is not simply a personal manifesto of what you hope to achieve with your child care center. It will be used to apply for grant money and entice investors to get excited about the opportunities you are giving to the families in your target area. Therefore, your business plan should include information about you and the best way to get ahold of you.

When writing your biography, you don't have to write what would equate to a short chapter in a novel. Instead keep it short and sweet, while hitting on key points. Below is a wonderful example of how you could fashion your biographical information:

Lisa Pennington is a recognized leader in the child care industry. She has provided exceptional home child care services to children since 2004. In 2009, Ms. Pennington began offering continuing education to child care workers to ensure that children in all communities are being cared for by trained staff. Ms. Pennington certifies applicants as directors and daycare works and also provides CPR-First Aid-AED training. She is licensed in the state of Texas.

You can reach Ms. Pennington using the following contact information:

Lisa's Little Ones
214.474.0017
http://www.startmychild carebusiness.com

HIRING A BUSINESS PLAN WRITER

Should you hire a business plan writer? This is a question I hear frequently from child care center owners I work with. My answer is always, "Absolutely!" You'll never go wrong working with a professional that understand the intricacies and the value of a detailed business plan. I help child care professionals every day write detailed business plans that get results because I understand the particular needs of the child industry.

Remember, a roadmap is only as good as it is drawn. If you can't understand the directions or it points you in the wrong way, you'll end up lost on your journey.

KEY POINTS FROM CHAPTER 2

Successful businesses, both large and small, use their business plans to help them identify their competition, their strengths and weaknesses, and other factors that will have a direct effect on how their well they can expect their business to profit.

A business plan points you in the right direction to economic sustainability; however, it also gives you a deeper understanding of the nuts and bolts of not only your business, but of your industry.

The executive summary portion of your business plan should make a stellar, first impression. A well-written executive summary demonstrates that you have a clear understanding of what needs are not being met within your target audience and how your child care center can fill this void.

The only way to run a lucrative child care business is to know how much money is coming into the center at all times. Accounting and cash flow are two main requirements of any business plan. It is what funders and investors will analyze to make sure you have the means to support your financial requests.

CHAPTER 3
Increase Your Child Care Center's Wealth as a Non-Profit Organization
How to Make a Profit as a 501(c)(3) Child Care Center

Lisa Pennington

INTRODUCTION

One of the biggest myths in business is that you have to operate as a for-profit organization in order to attain any sort of financial success. A for-profit business structure may look great on paper, but in an industry inundated with child care providers operating in this manner, choosing this path could actually limit your ability to compete in the marketplace.

Let's take a moment to examine how for-profit child care centers make their money...

These centers are reliant on parent fees to operate. When your provider costs increase, where are you going to get the money to make up the difference? You have two choices: raise rates or cut programs. This is a lose-lose situation. Parents are already paying large sums of money every week for quality child care. While raising your rates slightly may not raise any eyebrows, if the rate increase is substantial, you'll start to lose families to child care centers that charge considerably less.

On the flipside, let's say you keep your rates the same and choose to eliminate certain programs like before and after school care, or you stop buying new learning materials and recycle the same lesson plans over and over again. Instead of eliminating programs, you may opt to put off repairs. These choices could cause parents to pull their children from your center in favor of a child care center that has the ability to offer the best educational programs without compromising their children's safety. The residual effects of cutting programs and/or services could have a lasting effect on your child care center's reputation in the community.

Child care center operators are faced with tough choices every day. The goal is to find balance. Operating your business as a non-profit, 501(c)(3) organization is an innovative way to achieve this objective.

In this chapter, I'll explain the benefits of shaping your child care business as a 501(c)(3) organization and what steps you need to take for the IRS to recognize your non-profit, tax-exempt status (yes, tax-exempt – this is considered by many to be the major benefit of non-profit status), and how your center can make more money as a non-profit than a for-profit business by applying for funding exclusively reserved for 501(c)(3) organizations, accepting charitable donations, and reducing your tax liability.

THE NUTS AND BOLTS OF NON-PROFIT 501(c)(3) STATUS

Let's start by examining the definition of 501(c)(3) status. Non-profit businesses must abide by certain rules. When you file as a non-profit entity with the IRS, your business must meet and agree to the following qualifications:

- The organization must be organized and operated exclusively for exempt purposes set forth in section 501(c)(3) of the IRS tax code
- Earning of the non-profit shall not be shared among a single owner, partner, shareholders, employees, etc.
- All assets, including intellectual property, belong to the nonprofit and not individuals working for the non-profit.
- Reasonable compensation can be given to employees in the form of a salary or hourly-wage as part of the operating costs.
- Monies made after operating costs have been paid must be reinvested back into the program and used for services.
- If a 501(c)(3) organization ceases operations, the remaining assets must be distributed to another tax exempt agency or to federal or state public programs.

At first glance, this may seem rather restrictive, especially if you started your child care business as a way to have control over your financial future, while providing a much needed service in your community. However, when you look at the big picture and realize all the doors that open to your business through exclusive funding, you'll quickly see that operating as a 501(c)(3) provides financial security and the opportunity to grow your center ten-fold.

Some of the benefits for you and your contributors, according to the IRS, when you're recognized as a 501(c)(3) organization are:

1. Exemption from federal and/or state corporate income taxes
2. Possible exemption from state sales and property taxes (varies by state)
3. Ability to apply for grants and other public or private allocations available only to IRS-recognized, 501(c)(3) organizations
4. Potentially higher thresholds before incurring federal and/or state unemployment tax liabilities
5. The public legitimacy of IRS recognition

For a child care center these benefits have the ability to help you save money and earn money simultaneously. It enables you to hire quality child care providers, trained teachers, certified directors, and provide exceptional programming to meet the needs of all the children in your community.

At the end of this chapter, I'll provide you with a short list of grants that 501(c)(3) child care centers are eligible to apply for. But, for now, let's take a moment to discuss how this non-profit status can help your center bring in more monetary donations and charitable contributions.

CHARITABLE DONATIONS

Grant money can help your non-profit child care center fund educational programs, make updates to your facilities, and offer additional benefits to the families and the children you serve. But, sometimes, grant money isn't enough to fill the gap when there is a shortage of funding. Some grants are one-time offers that are unavailable for renewal or you may work tirelessly to apply for funding only to be one of thousands of non-profits competing for limited funds.

What can you do to compensate for economic shortfalls when grant money isn't enough?

The easiest answer is to solicit charitable donations from your local community. These community partners could be businesses, faith-based organizations, service organizations, schools, and individual donors. If you need a substantial amount of funding to help you reach a financial goal for a new educational program or to make improvements to your classrooms, you need donors who are willing to open up their checkbooks and not hesitate to put a few zeros behind that initial number. When you offer tax advantages to these potential donors, you'll quickly discover that more and more businesses and individuals are willing to make significant financial contributions to your organization.

As a 501(c)(3) organization you can solicit for donations and provide your donors with a tax receipt that can be used to deduct all or a portion of their donation on their income tax returns. The exact amount of what they can deduct will be dependent on their own tax situation and any donors with questions should always be directed to speak with their financial advisor for specifics regarding their situation.

Child care centers that have the ability to accept tax-deductible contributions can feel confident soliciting help from community partners. Not only are these donations helping your center grow and thrive, but you are offering your contributors an invaluable tax benefit that will encourage them to continue to respond to your request for financial assistance in the future.

HOW TO FIND AND APPLY FOR GRANTS

A grant is monetary support provided by public or private organizations that does not need to be paid back since it is not a loan. However, unlike loans, grant money must be spent according to the program guidelines of the particular funding program. For example, if you apply for a grant through the Child and Adult Care Food Program, any money your child care organization receives must be used for nutritional-related expenses or specific items as outlines in the particular grant you've applied for.

Grants are wonderful ways to fund new and exciting programs in your center that attract families in need of high quality daycare. Depending on the type of funding you receive, a grant may be able to help your center with the following:

Cover the costs of child care for low-income families

- Purchase food for the center
- Assist with the purchase of educational or learning materials
- Purchase safe playground equipment
- Upgrade facilities
- Expand or relocate your facility
- Train staff

Finding grants is relatively easy to do. In a moment, I'll share with you a list of grant resources that you may want to investigate further to see if there are programs that will benefit your center. The tricky part is applying for the money and meeting the criteria set by the organization disbursing the money. Just because you have 501(c)(3) status doesn't automatically make your center eligible for all grants. In some cases, you may have to apply to be part of a program first before you can apply for grant money for individual funding opportunities.

A great example of one such program is the Head Start program. This is a nationally-recognized program that provides free developmental and learning services to children from low-income families beginning at birth through age five. Child care centers that are part of the Head Start program are given tools and resources to help with the child's emotional, mental, and social development to prepare them for kindergarten. In addition, Head Start has a number of opportunities for child care centers to apply for additional funding to further improve their center's offerings, facilities, and the training of staff. However, these funding opportunities are only available to centers that are recognized as Head Start centers.

When applying for grants, it is important to read through all the qualifiers to make sure you meet the criteria and do not waste time applying for funds that you are not eligible for. The following are a few examples of how grants are awarded:

- Location
- Programs offered
- Age of children
- Years in business
- Tax-exempt status
- Staff credentials

In addition to meeting all the qualifiers, you also have to pay attention to the filing deadlines. Most grant programs do not operate on a rolling basis. This means that you will be required to have all information filled out and submitted within a certain time period to qualify. Applications received after this period will not be considered until the next grant period or not at all. It depends on the individual grant.

Likewise, all grants require different information. When researching and applying for grants, you must take the time to read the fine print. Request grant toolbox kits if one is available for the funding opportunity you're applying for. These toolbox kits will list everything you need to include with your application to make sure your center qualifies.

Don't miss a step. Forgetting to include a copy of your licensing or a copy of your 501(c)(3) status or even forgetting to sign the application can result in an automatic denial.

Should I hire a grant writer?

This is a question that a lot of child care center operators ask. Many grant applications are available online and are seemingly simple to complete, especially if you have your business plan nearby.

Remember that business plan we talked about earlier? It comes in handy when applying for grant money. But, sometimes, your business plan isn't enough. If you're not familiar with grant writing language, if your writing skills aren't quite polished, or you don't have the time needed to put into writing a compelling application, then you should consider hiring a grant writer. These individuals know what language needs to be included in your application to get the attention it deserves.

The cost for a grant writer varies depending on the type of grant and amount of work involved. However, I urge you to think about the return on your investment.

Spending a fair amount of money on grant writing services will give you a leg up on the competition and the money you receive from the funding opportunity will almost always outweigh the money you pay for professional grant writing resources.

One thing to consider when hiring a grant writer is to make sure he or she will submit the grant for you. Not all grant writers include this service. If you do not have knowledge about how to submit a grant, you'll want to find a writer that offers submission as part of his or her services.

GRANT RESOURCES

There are hundreds of opportunities for child care funding through both public programs and private foundations or companies. Unfortunately, I can't possibly list them all. The small list that follows is comprised of resources I have personally used or programs that have numerous funding opportunities on a larger scale. I also suggest that you spend time researching online for funding opportunities that are local as well as statewide.

Don't be afraid to try for smaller grants. These grants, which tend to be local grants, usually have a smaller pool of applicants and are easier to qualify for. Receiving many small grants can provide your center with just as much financial assistance as larger grants.

The grant resources listed in this section should be

investigated thoroughly before applying for any funding. You'll want to view their list of requirements as they may frequently change. Some of the resources are for national or state programs, while other resources are for smaller projects.

Disclaimer: Some of the program descriptions were copied directly from the organization's website and I did not receive any sort of compensation for providing you with this information.

Child and Adult Care Food Program

Food & Nutrition Service
3101 Park Center Drive
Alexandria, VA 22302
http://www.fns.usda.gov

Programs funded by the Food and Nutrition Service are administered at the state and local levels. Child care center operators will want to visit the website provided above to find contact information for their particular state's program information.

The Child Care and Development Fund

Administration for Children and Families
370 L'Enfant Promenade, S.W.
Washington, D.C. 20447
Phone: (202) 690-6782
Fax: (202) 690-5600
http://www.acf.hhs.gov/programs/occ

Helps states, territories, and federally recognized tribes and tribal organizations provide child care for low-income families and increase the affordability and quality of child care and development services. Contact the administration offices for funding requests and information.

Dollar General Foundation Grants Program

http://www.grantsoffice.com/GrantDetails.aspx?gid=26496

The Dollar General Foundation offers a number of grants to improve literacy such as the Beyond Words Program and the Youth Literacy Program. Visit the website mentioned above for a full list of the criteria, funding amounts, and application deadlines.

The Foundation Centre

http://foundationcenter.org/

This independent service organization is a wonderful resource for foundation and corporate giving. You can access a large amount of information related to child care funding by typing in "child care grants" in the search bar.

Head Start

(866) 763-6481
HeadStart@eclkc.info
http://eclkc.ohs.acf.hhs.gov/hslc/grants

The Office of Head Start (OHS) awards grant funding and provides oversight to the agencies that deliver Head Start services. OHS uses a competitive process to award grants. Under the Designation Renewal System (DRS), Head Start grants are awarded for a five year project period. The Applicant Support and Early Head Start-Child Care Partnerships toolkits support those interested in applying for grant funding.

Home Depot's Community Grant Programs

2455 Paces Ferry Road, Atlanta, GA 30339
Tel (770) 384-3889
hd_foundation@homedepot.com
http://www.homedepotfoundation.org/

Home Depot's grant programs can provide funding opportunities to help you improve your facility. Grants, up to $5,000, are available to IRS-registered 501(c)(3) designated organizations and tax-exempt public service agencies in the U.S. that are using the power of volunteers to improve the physical health of their community. Grants are given in the form of The Home Depot gift cards for the purchase of tools, materials, or services.

State Grant Opportunities

http://www.k12grants.org/Grants

This is a privately operated Internet resource for individuals seeking state funding. The website provides links to state education departments and other sources.

TEACH

info@teach.com
http://teach.com/

Teaching grants can fund professional development, classroom enrichment, school supplies, field trips and almost anything else that goes into bettering the quality of education.

U.S. Department of Education

400 Maryland Avenue, SW
Washington, D.C. 20202
(800) USA-LEARN
http://www2.ed.gov/fund/grants-apply.html

The U.S. Department of Education awards discretionary grants to public and private organizations to help with training programs, recreational programs, comprehensive center programs, and much more. The amounts vary and certain restrictions apply. Grants are available to nonprofit as well as for-profit educational programs depending on the particular grant.

Walmart Community Grant Program

http://foundation.walmart.com/apply-for-grants/

Walmart's Community Grant Program focuses on the following initiatives: Hunger Relief and Healthy Eating,

Sustainability, Career Opportunity, Women's Economic Empowerment, and Special Interests. Following the link provided above will send you directly to Walmart's community giving site where you will find information and guidelines about the various funding opportunities.

GRANT WRITING SCAMS

Before I wrap up this section, I want to warn you about grant writing scams. Unfortunately, there are people out there that are only interested in ripping you off. Therefore, you need to be very wary of any grant writing company that promises or requires the following:

- Guarantees that you'll get the grant you're applying for. No one can make these guarantees.
- Asks for fees upfront. While it is customary for a company to ask for a small amount up front to begin the process, the entirety of the fee should only be paid once the grant is written.

Lastly, when you're applying for a grant, never pay large sums of money to submit an application. Grant applications rarely ask for money upfront and those that do should be avoided because they are most likely scams.

KEY POINTS FROM CHAPTER 3

Operating as a 501(c)(3) provides financial security and the opportunity to grow your center ten-fold.

Grant money can help your non-profit child care center fund educational programs, make updates to your facilities, and offer additional benefits to the families and the children you serve.

When applying for funding, make sure you request guidelines and application kits from the funding source. Review the funding guidelines and make sure your child care center and the program you're interested in funding meets the requirements. Contact the funding agency directly with any questions you may have.

Consider hiring a grant writer to assist you with preparing your proposal, cover letter, and any other parts of the grant application.

Grant applications rarely ask for money upfront and

those that do should be avoided because they are most likely scams.

Lisa Pennington

CHAPTER 4
Train for Success
Training and Staffing Concerns

INTRODUCTION

Profitable child care facilities maximize their profits by applying for grants and receiving vouchers or payments from federal and/or state subsidy programs. Managing your bottom line in this manner allows you to offer the highest quality child care possible without increasing rates. Child care providers that rely on grant and subsidy funding are able to serve all families in the area including at-risk, low-income families. When your child care center is able to offer services to a broad sector of the community, you corner the market and the potential for profit is limitless.

But there is a catch.

You may be a wonderful grant writer, or you may hire an accomplished grant writer. You may know how to find hidden money and access funding that no one else is able to find. However, if your staff lacks credentials and is not trained properly you won't qualify for a single cent of this money.

When applying for grants and federal subsidies, you already know that your child care center must have valid licensure, copies of full criminal background checks and child abuse checks for your employees. But did you know that you must also show proof that your staff members have the proper credentials and adequate training to care for the children in your program? In many circumstances, you'll need proof in the form of certification that your director (whether that is you or another person you've hired) has the education and know-how to run a functioning, profitable, and compliant child care center.

Small child care centers going up against established child care conglomerates need to be able to compete for the grants or subsidies they are applying for. The best way to accomplish this is to make sure that every single employee hired by your child care organization is highly trained now and in the future. It isn't enough to train someone once. You need to make sure that your employees are receiving the latest information to ensure that the children are exposed to a well-rounded learning environment. Your director, assistant director, and other management staff need to consistently reevaluate their skills and make improvements based on new child care management techniques and directives.

Staffing concerns are something that many child care centers, both large and small, deal with. High turnover in the child care industry is common. This is usually due to low pay, lack of benefits, lack of education, and lack of proper management. Many child care center owners fail to understand the direct effect a poorly trained and unhappy staff has on the profitability of their center. Owners who address these issues head-on will find that they retain well-educated staff and can access the funds needed to pay these employees what they are worth.

During this chapter we'll explore how to keep your employees properly trained to make your center eligible for exclusive grants and subsidies. I'll introduce you to programs such as Train the Trainer and explain the benefits of the Child Development Associate (CDA) Credential. We will also examine the differences between the CDA credential and a Director's Certificate.

Whether you're just starting out on your child care journey or you've been on the path for a while but are feeling a little lost, this valuable information will help you lay the foundation for a child care center that is well-staffed and qualified to receive the most desired child care subsidies in the industry on federal, state, and local levels.

TRAIN THE TRAINER

What is Train the Trainer? How can participating in one of these programs benefit my center? As a childcare specialist and consultant, these are questions I am asked all the time by childcare center operators who are curious about how this specific model of teaching and learning can improve the skills of their employees to better the programs for the children and families being served.

Let's begin with the first question: What is Train the Trainer?

Training requirements for childcare providers and educators are constantly being tweaked. In order to meet the requirements of your state's licensing board or to comply with the funding conditions of grants or subsidies, it is necessary for your employees to continue to have access to quality resources that will help them acquire and retain certain skills and knowledge pertaining to the care and education of the children at your center. These training requirements, while well intentioned, can be met with certain obstacles:

- ➢ Employees may not be able to attend trainings because they are not available in the area.
- ➢ Employees may not have the funds to pay for trainings and the center may not be able to reimburse the cost.

> Employees may not be able to devote the time outside of normal work hours to attend trainings that are not offered at convenient hours.

These hurdles can dramatically affect the quality of your staff and disqualify your center for certain funding opportunities. Train the Trainer programs offer a solution.

These programs are designed to teach experienced and educated childcare providers how to present childcare-related curriculum to lesser-educated employees in a fun and engaging manner that is compliant with the educational requirements set forth by state licensing laws and funding requirements.

Break it down for me. How can these programs help me increase my center's cash flow and profitability?

As a childcare center director, you're automatically qualified to teach the employees of your own center. But, what if you own two centers? Did you know that even though you own both locations, you're only allowed to teach the employees at the location you physically oversee? The benefits of having qualified trainers on your team means you can offer your employees at your other locations quality continuing education credits without requiring them to travel long distances, spend their hard-earned money on classes, and give up their free time. But these aren't the only benefits.

You can help other childcare providers achieve the same

goals by offering your services for a fee. As a childcare provider, your main objective should always be to provide the best possible care for the children at your center. One of the surest ways to offer the highest quality of care is to have an operating budget that allows you to add programs and services that consistently improve the curriculum of your early childhood education offerings and the general care of the children in your program. However, one of the greatest challenges that childcare centers face – as I've already previously mentioned – is generating enough cash flow to make this happen.

Becoming a registered trainer in your state not only enables you to offer low-cost or free trainings to your staff at multiple locations, but you can offer your services to other centers in the area. When you're paid to train other childcare workers, you're generating income that can be put back into your business and used to improve your program's services, keeping you one step ahead of the competition.

How do I become a trainer and get registered?

Let's take this step-by-step.

1. You must complete an approved Train the Trainer course. You can find these courses online, through a local community college, or by contacting the Early Childhood Education accrediting authority in your state. You can also contact me directly at (214) 474-0017. I offer a Train the Trainer course through my website

www.startmychildcarebusiness.com and can point you in the right direction. You can also contact me directly at (214) 474-0017. I offer a Train the Trainer course through my website www.startmychildcarebusiness.com.

3. Review the requirements to become a certified trainer in your state. Again, each state has different requirements. If you have an Associate's Degree, Bachelor's Degree, or Graduate Degree in Early Childhood Education or a relevant field of study, you may automatically qualify to register as a trainer after you have completed an approved Train the Trainer course. But, in some cases, you may be required to complete a certain number of credit hours or their clock hour equivalent to qualify as a trainer. For example, in the state of Texas, the following requirements apply:

- High School Diploma or GED and completion of 12 credit hours of Early Childhood or Child Development courses (or its clock hour equivalent of 192 clock hours of training)
- High School Diploma or GED and Early Childhood certification (current and valid)
- Associate's Degree in a related field to Early Childhood/Child Development and completion of 12 credit hours of Early Childhood or Child Development courses (or its clock hour equivalent of 192 clock hours of training)
- Associate's Degree in Early Childhood/Child Development
- Bachelor's Degree in a related field to Early Childhood/Child Development and completion

of 12 credit hours of Early Childhood or Child Development courses (or its clock hour equivalent of 192 clock hours of training)
- Bachelor's Degree in Early Childhood/Child Development
- Graduate Degree in a related field to Early Childhood/Child Development and completion of 12 credit hours of Early Childhood or Child Development courses (or its clock hour equivalent of 192 clock hours of training)
- Graduate Degree in Early Childhood/Child Development

This information is taken directly from the Revised Educational Qualifications for the Texas Trainer Registry, last updated January of 2012. Your state's requirements may be different. I cannot stress this point enough.

4. Consider the eligibility of your clock hours. Clock hours must be earned within a certain period of time. For example, to register as a trainer with the Texas Trainer Registry, clock hours must be taken within a 3 year period.

5. Clock hours will only be accepted if they were earned while participating in trainings or courses taught by administrators, state agencies, or other professionals in early childhood as outlined according to your state's requirements.

6. A person's years of experience in early childhood education is also taken into consideration when

completing the registration process.

Train the Trainer programs are invaluable to the profitability of your childcare center, both in terms of gaining a more educated staff that will qualify your center for funding and helping you generate additional income for your center.

Every day I am surprised just how many childcare providers are unaware of this amazing opportunity for growth and financial success. If there is one thing you do today for your center's economic growth, check into learning as much as you can about Train the Trainer programs in your state.

MANAGEMENT CREDENTIALS

There are many reasons why a person may start out in the childcare industry:

- A stay-at-home parent wants to earn money to support his or her family
- An individual sees a need in the community and has a desire to fills the gaps
- Entrepreneurs who take a keen interest in the childcare industry and want to bring quality education to children and families in the community

Whatever your reason may be for operating a childcare center, it is only as good as its leadership. We've already established that in order to run a successful business and to qualify for competitive grants and limited subsidies that your staff must be highly trained and properly credentialed. But, what about you? As the director, you are the anchor of the organization. Without the proper management credentials, your center will sink and take everyone down with it.

This is why it's important to look at what steps you need to take as a childcare center director to make sure you're taken seriously. You can do this in one of two ways. You can take classes to receive a Director's Certificate or earn a Child Development Associate (CDA) credential.

In this section, we'll take a closer look at what these two management credentials mean for you and the success and overall profitability of your center. Remember, when you invest in yourself, you invest in your business. It's a win-win situation.

The Director's Certificate

Before I begin to explain a little about the Director's Certificate program and its learning objectives, it's important to keep a few things in mind. Like with any of the other examples in this book, the specifics of these courses may be slightly altered depending on the state where you live. As a licensed childcare director and consultant in the state of Texas, the majority of my examples will be based off of the Texas Director's Certificate requirements. For specific requirements related to your state, visit the Childcare Education Institute or speak with educational counselors through early childhood education programs in your state to learn the exact requirements of your state's particular Director Certificate requirements.

So, without any further ado, let's get started . . .

What is the point of a Director's Certificate, you may ask?

Some people have a business background and they think that getting into the childcare business really isn't all that different, but it is. Whether you have a business background or you're wet behind the ears when it comes to managing a thriving childcare operation, you have to understand certain key components of the industry. A quality Director's Certificate program will help you do this. By the completion of the course, you should have a deeper appreciate and knowledge of child growth and development as well as business management.

The program you choose, whether it is an online certificate program or a program taught in a traditional classroom setting, will have its own ways of accessing your comprehension and understanding of these topics. Some courses will require short writing assignments and student activities with written feedback, while others may rely on multiple choice style questions or true and false tests. However, nearly all will require quizzes and some kind of formal, final exam.

Program lengths vary, too. The Director's Certificate course I teach is a 40 hour course and includes topics such as the following:

- Child Care Regulations
- Business Management and Professional Development
- Finances and Fiscal Management
- Community Resources and Services
- Developmentally Appropriate Practice
- Parent Education
- Ethical Program Development

Most individuals who take the class can finish it in a weekend, but you are allowed six months to complete the course. This is one of the easiest and surest ways to improve your credentials.

Child Development Associate (CDA) Credential

If you're searching for a child care credential that is highly recognized and accepted at face value throughout the United States, the CDA Credential checks all the right boxes. For those looking to take their career in early childhood education one step farther, the CDA credential is a natural stepping stone to career advancement.

Child care providers who want to give their parents peace of mind, and highlight their commitment to provide quality child care services, find that the CDA credential adds strength to their program and their own personal, academic, and management credentials. CDA students learn the importance implementing CDA Competency Standards in their programs. The Standards are a set of goals that are designed to educate the whole child, provide a safe environment, and strengthen the relationship between caregiver and parent. Taken directly from the CDA website, here are the six Competency Standards of the CDA program:

- To establish and maintain a safe and healthy learning environment
- To advance physical and intellectual competence
- To support social and emotional development and to provide positive guidance
- To establish positive and productive relationships with families
- To ensure a well-run, purposeful program responsive to participant needs
- To maintain a commitment to professionalism

The CDA Credential is available for child care providers that offer center-based preschool care, center-based infant care, family care, and home visit programs. However, the CDA is not an umbrella credential that automatically endorses or certifies a single person in all these areas. For example, if you want to be CDA credentialed to provide center-based preschool care and be CDA credentialed to operate a home visit program for families that are not seeking traditional preschool childcare, you will need to complete two separate programs.

Which One Is Better – A Director's Certificate or a CDA?

It all depends on three things:

- Your overall early childhood education goals
- The amount of time you want to spend on the course
- Future funding plans

Both the Director's Certificate and the CDA credential will give credence to your child care operation, but you cannot operate a daycare with just the CDA. The CDA can be earned separately or along with a 15 hour child growth and development course track from a community college program.

Whichever path you choose, you'll have the educational background that will let funders and parents know that you are not merely a babysitter. You will have the experience and knowledge to run and operate a successful center that is capable of delivering the quality of care that today's parents expect of their children's child care providers.

Regardless of which on one you choose, you're:

- Investing in your company's future;
- Increasing your company's effectiveness, and
- Ensuring that you'll be able to offer a program that will support competitive tuition rates

The Director's Certificate is ideal for child care providers that are interested in the administration of early childhood education programs. If you plan to take an active role in the day-to-day operations and fiscal responsibilities, the Director's Certificate is a shorter program, requiring fewer credit hours, and can be earned slightly quicker than the CDA credential.

The CDA credential is a more complete program that examines the role of the caregiver and how his or her interactions with the children, parents, and the community can create an early education environment that educates and nurtures the whole child. Emphasis is not placed so much on administration as it is on the emotional, social, and physical well-being of the children being serviced and running a purposeful program.

If you're interested in learning more about the CDA credential, a wonderful resource is the Council for Professional Recognition. By visiting their website, which is listed in the resources at the end of this chapter, you'll have direct access to all your questions about the CDA credential.

STAFFING CONCERNS

A well-trained staff is wonderful because it ensures the children in your care are receiving the proper attention and education, but what good is a well-trained staff if you can't stop the high rate of turnover that so many child care centers fall victim to?

Why do child care centers have such a low retention rate? This common problem can be attributed to the following four "Ls":

- Low pay
- Lack of benefits
- Lack of education
- Lack of proper management

Parents are frequently concerned about the high turnover rates in child care centers across the United States. In fact, it's one of the main reasons that parents pull their children from one daycare to another.

High turnover rates hurt everyone and low retention rates make child care centers look bad. It creates a never ending cycle of constant hiring and training. Children that attend centers with high turnover rates may refuse to go to school. They may have trouble forming bonds with their teachers or child care providers because the faces of the staff keep changing.

The key to retaining qualified staff is to assure that your teachers receive pay that matches their education, training, and experience. This is why I encourage child care center operators to hire staff members that have the proper credentials and/or degrees necessary to qualify for the best funding sources possible. This is the best way to ensure that your staff is always paid what they're worth. Employees who feel adequately compensated for the time and effort they put into their careers are employees that won't always be looking for a better job.

You can also encourage your lesser educated employees to further their training by looking into programs that offer the following benefits:

- Grant programs designed to compensate teachers and child care providers based on their educational level.
- Scholarship programs that offer a salary increase when teachers reach certain educational milestones.
- Increased reimbursement rates for child care services that continuously improve their quality of care.

But great pay isn't always enough . . .

We also have to address the lack of benefits for part-time and full-time child care educators. You may compensate your educators according to industry standards, but are you giving them the benefits they need most like paid time-off to care for themselves and family members when they become ill? What about medical and dental benefits? Do your educators get paid vacation time to regroup and reenergize without worrying about losing a week's worth of pay?

When educators have respectable benefits, they feel valued. They are more likely to be satisfied with their jobs, arrive on time, and have fewer "sick" days.

A wonderful resource that I recommend to child care managers in need of affordable benefit plans for their employees is Dental Plans.com. Don't let the name fool you. The company offers dental plans as well as vision and prescription plans. Employers can customize dental, vision, and prescription needs into a personalized plan for individual employees for a low monthly rate. Depending on your child care center's financial situation, you can choose to pay the entire monthly rate for your employees or pay a portion and take the rest out of your employees' paychecks to cover the rest.

Child care providers who use the promo code **CHILDCARE10** ***get three months free!***

Another way to offer comprehensive benefits to your employees is to work hard to get other programs in your center paid for through grants and subsidies. For example, earlier in the book, I talked about the Child and Adult Care Food Program. This subsidy reimburses child care centers for their nutritional costs. With your center's food costs covered you could have extra money to spend on other benefits for your employees.

Lastly, let's talk about management style...

If your center is already offering amazing benefits and your employees are properly compensated for their education experience, but you're still experiencing high turnover rates, the problem could be with your management style.

Ask yourself the following questions:

- Do I listen to my employees' concerns?
- Do I have an open door policy?

- Do I communicate policies and procedures in a concise and understandable manner?
- Do I respect my employees' time away from the center?

Management that doesn't make it easy for their employees to voice concerns or offer opinions are often viewed as dictators. While you are in charge of the center and its day-to-day operations, your educators are often on the front lines. They see things and can identify problems within the facility that you may have overlooked and don't know exist. Employees that feel that they are contributing to their work environment feel respected and part of the team.

Child care center managers have a lot on their plates and sometimes communication can break down. If you're constantly changing policies and procedures without adequately informing your staff, tensions and division between management and educators can develop. Lack of communication is a major player in an employee's decision to resign and seek employment elsewhere. Always make the time to communicate with your educators.

Lastly, are you constantly requiring members of your staff to stay late for meetings or to fill in for others? Do you schedule meetings afterhours or on weekends on a regular basis?

I don't have to tell you how hard it is to run a child care

organization. Even if you're a small center, you know the challenges. But, those challenges shouldn't interfere with your employees' time away from work. Afterhours and weekend training sessions may be necessary every once and a while, but don't make them a weekly habit. When you do need to schedule these trainings, let your employees know well in advance.

Also, when hiring new employees, if additional training sessions are mandatory throughout the year, let the new hire know this before they choose to come on board. This will save you the headache of losing a staff member several weeks down the line because they didn't fully understand their obligations when accepting your job offer.

KEY POINTS FROM CHAPTER 4

Small childcare centers going up against established childcare conglomerates need to be able to compete for the grants or subsidies they are applying for. The best way to accomplish this is to make sure that every single employee hired by your childcare organization is highly trained now and in the future.

To meet the requirements of your state's licensing board or to comply with the funding conditions of grants or subsidies, it is necessary for your employees to continue to have access to quality resources that will help them acquire and retain certain skills and knowledge pertaining to the care and education of the children at your center.

Becoming a registered trainer in your state not only enables you to offer low-cost or free trainings to your staff at multiple locations, but you can offer your services to other centers in the area. When you're paid to train other childcare workers, you're generating income that can be put back into your business and used to improve your program's services.

The Director's Certificate is ideal for child care providers that are interested in the administration of early childhood education programs.

The CDA credential is a complete program that examines the role of the caregiver and how his or her interactions with the children, parents, and the community can create an early education environment that educates and nurtures the whole child.

Low pay, lack of benefits, lack of education, and lack of proper management contribute to high turnover rates for child care centers.

Lisa Pennington

CHAPTER 5
<u>Profitable Management Strategies</u>
Overcoming Financial Obstacles

INTRODUCTION

Relying on funding and subsidies is not enough to keep a child care organization in the black. While these resources can make up a significant portion of your business' revenue, it is critical that you continue to do everything you can to generate income and pay close attention to how the money is used that comes into your center.

In this chapter, I'll discuss common obstacles that child care centers face that on the surface do not seem detrimental to the bottom line, but can have a huge impact on a business' profitability. These obstacles include the following:

- Periods of low enrollment
- Handling parent complaints
- Safeguarding your center's reputation
- Dealing with local competition
- Fiscal management issues such as dealing with non-payment for services and collecting on bad checks

Every single child care provider will face these challenges at one time or another. The goal is to not be blindsided, but to have a plan to deal with these situations as they arise.

HOW TO DEAL WITH LOW ENROLLMENT

Some child care businesses start off slow, gaining new children a little at a time. Other organizations are intended to be massive undertakings from the very beginning. Whether you're a small, home-based center or a larger child care operation, you rely on the tuition or fees you receive. When your enrollment drops, this can significantly affect your businesses income and your ability to pay your employees.

Enrollment ebbs and flows with the economic conditions in the community your center serves. It is also affected by the birth rates. For example, during the recession that hit the nation hard between 2007 and 2009, more and more people were delaying having children. The result of the decision by so many families to hold off increasing the size of their families led to a decrease in child care enrollments in the subsequent years.

You are not psychic. You cannot foretell the future. If you were, you'd predict the numbers for the next lottery drawing and you wouldn't need this book, right? As business owners, we cannot predict with certainty how well our business will do in the future. However, with a little luck and a lot of planning, we can take certain measures to make sure our centers don't falter when economic conditions threaten our business' livelihood.

Whether you're a new program or a center that has been operating in the community for years, the following suggestions can help you keep enrollment steady.

Advertise

You don't need to spend a fortune on advertising. You don't need to rent a highway billboard or pay for print or radio ads. While these are wonderful ways to spread the word about your center, sometimes these methods simply aren't in the budget or may not make the most sense for your business. Instead, consider the following ideas:

- Hold quarterly or bi-annually open house events. These events introduce families to your center in a relaxed, laid-back, no pressure atmosphere. Spend money on family friendly food and treats, set up a bounce house, or have a family movie night with a projector set up in the outside play area of your center. Make the event free and open to the public. During the event, offer discounted registration for parents that sign up the same day and ask parents to sign up for your email list.
- Email lists are equivalent to the tried and true waiting list, but better. Not only will you have a list of potential families to send vacancy information to when a spot at your center needs to be filled, but you can send newsletters and other information about what is happening at your center throughout the year. Keeping the

lines of communication constantly open with prospective families and showing them just how great your center is encourages prospective families to jump at the first opportunity to enroll their child when it presents itself.

- Participate in community events. Parades are great community events that can give your business the exposure it needs and you don't even have to spend the time and money on a fancy float. Many parades are simply happy to have local businesses walk in the parade and hand out candy or favors like beads, fans, water bottles, and even popsicles. When handing out these items to parade-goers, make sure you have a couple staff members walking on either side of the procession handing out flyers with your center's information to parents in the crowd. This form of advertising is not only dirt cheap, but fun!
- Leave flyers and other information on bulletin boards. Grocery stores, fax and mailing centers, libraries, and coffee shops are local establishments that are usually very happy to help you advertise. Again, the only cost is printing expenses.

HOW TO HANDLE PARENT COMPLAINTS AND SAFEGUARD YOUR CENTER'S REPUTATION

Here's the thing. As a business owner, you're going to hear complaints. Some of these complaints are warranted, while others are simply the rantings and ravings of people who don't feel they get the attention they think they deserve. However, no matter what your personal opinion on the matter may be, you must take all parent complaints seriously.

No one likes to be on the receiving end of an angry parent. Not only does it make a person defensive, but it can cause you to lose confidence in yourself and your business strategy. But, the single most damaging thing you can do to your business and its reputation in the community is to not accept and take action when complaints are filed.

Dismissing a parent's complaint sends the message that you don't care. When this happens, parents talk. They talk on the playground about how inefficient your center is. They bad-mouth your management style on social media. They stand around at school dismissal and pick apart your staff members.

Word of mouth not only builds a center up, it can also tear it down.

Here are a few strategies you may want to try to keep parent complaints in check:

- Always listen politely when a parent comes to you with a concern. Use a loving and compassionate tone with the parent. Most complaints can easily be solved with a smile and the promise to look into the situation.
- Teach employees to praise the child before speaking with him or her about the problem. This

- Follow up with the parent and give them an actual date of when you will follow up. If you say you're going to look into the matter, then make sure you follow through with your promise and provide the parent with feedback. For example, if a parent says her child wasn't allowed to sleep with his or her stuffed lamb at naptime, ask the child's teacher for his or her version of what happened. Go back to the parent with the teacher's response to the complaint. If necessary, arrange for a time to have all parties sit down and talk about the problem.
- Never bring the child into the middle of a parent/center dispute. Even if the child's behavior is the issue, remember that your role is to make all children in your center feel safe; not ridiculed or singled out. Speak privately with the parent.
- Keep an open door policy. Make sure you're available to speak to parents when they arrive to drop off and pick up their children.
- If the state becomes involved in the dispute, keep calm. Never get defensive with state authorities and always be willing to provide the information requested.

HOW TO DEAL WITH COMPETING CHILD CARE CENTERS

The child care industry is competitive. Centers that thrive are the ones that know how to handle the competition.

The first thing every business owner needs to know is they can't be everything to everyone. Trying to supersede every center in your community will stretch your resources thin. The ideal way to handle the competition is to do the following:

- Create a strong mission statement and base programming around the goals in your statement.
- Determine the needs of your community and fill the gap with quality child care services.
- Figure out what your niche and do it better than anyone else in the community.
- Price your services accordingly. Don't be tempted to offer child care too cheaply to compete. When you recognize the value in your services, your families will recognize it too.
- Seek out public and private funding sources to help you pay for operation costs to keep tuition low for your families.
- Make sure your center is clean and safe and always follow through with requests made by state inspection boards. The last thing you want is for your center to be blackballed in the community because of a bad safety report.

Most importantly is to focus on making your business the best it can be and don't spend too much time comparing yourself to other centers. Too many business owners pay too much attention to what their competition is doing and this can make them doubt what their business brings to the community. Stay on track and make sure your business is always represented in the best light possible.

This is the surest way to operate a profitable child care business.

HOW TO ADDRESS FISCAL MANAGEMENT CONCERNS

Every business owner, at some point in time, is going to have to address fiscal concerns such as non-payment for services and returned checks. It's tempting, especially for managers or owners that tend to be shy about asking for payment, to let a missed payment go every now and then. But, when you fall into this habit, you're putting your entire operation at financial risk.

You work hard to provide valuable child care services for your families. You are responsible for paying your employees. You are accountable for managing a safe and functional facility. You cannot do this without income.

Most families are going to pay their child's tuition on time, but life can get busy and a parent may forget. Here are some ways you can help parents pay their tuition in a timely manner and keep the cash flowing into your center:

- Offer automatic tuition payments that are deducted from the responsible party's checking or savings account
- Accept credit card payments
- Offer discounted tuition rates for parents that pay in full for an entire year or even for several months at a time

- Place payment reminders on the front door of your center, by the sign in sheet, etc.

What happens if a parent pays and the check is returned?

This can be an awkward situation for everyone involved. The best way to start a conversation about a returned check is to send a friendly letter or make a courtesy phone call to the parent. Make sure this is done in private out of earshot from other families. Remember, you want to make sure your families feel respected at all times.

Refer to your returned check policy in the parent handbook. Do you have a returned check policy? If not, now is the time to get one. Your policy should state the following:

- How long the parent has to make good on the check
- What form of payment will be accepted?
- The return check fee
- Steps that will be taken if the center is not reimbursed for the bounced check

Most of the time a returned check is an accounting error on the part of the parent and will be cleared up in a timely manner. Unfortunately, though, there are times when a parent may refuse to pay and you have to let the family go. Or, the child never returns and payment is still outstanding. This doesn't mean that you can't still try to recoup the funds owed to you.

In cases like these, you'll want to contact the Prosecuting Attorney's office in your county to inquire about their check collection procedures. Most PA offices have a bad check unit that deals specifically with hot checks. You'll most likely need to provide the PA's office with the check, details about the transaction, the check writer's address, etc. Generally, the PA's office will try to collect the funds owed to you without taking the check writer to court. However, criminal prosecution is not out of the question. Most check writers will end up making good on a hot check rather than face jail time or fees.

KEY POINTS FROM CHAPTER 5

You don't need to spend a fortune on advertising. There are a number of low budget advertising tactics such as generating email lists, participating in community events, and hosting open houses that will get the word out about your center and help you circumvent low enrollment.

The single most damaging thing you can do to your business and its reputation in the community is to not accept and take action when parent complaints are filed.

The first thing every business owner needs to know is they can't be everything to everyone. Trying to supersede every center in your community will stretch your resources thin. Figure out what your niche in the industry is and do it better than anyone else in the community.

You don't have to accept non-payment from parents, especially when tuition checks are returned by the parent's bank. Your center has legal ways to recoup money lost from bad checks.

CONCLUSION

Running a successful child care businesses doesn't come from luck. It comes from hard work, perseverance, and the desire to constantly learn more about the industry. Business owners that continually research funding options and strive to improve their programming are the ones that build businesses that last even during times of economic downturns.

Protecting your personal assets by forming an LLC; developing a concise business plan that will act as your roadmap to success; researching and applying for grants and subsidies to reduce the cost of tuition while increasing your center's wealth; training your employees and financially rewarding them for reaching educational milestones and managing your business with an eye always on the future, are the surest ways to help you operate a profitable child care business in an oversaturated industry.

Are you in the process of selling your child care business?

Selling a business is complicated and you need someone on your side who knows how to effectively market your business. While a real estate agent can sell your home, you need a real estate broker to sell your business. If you're contemplating selling, give me a call or send me an email to learn more about how my proven selling strategies can help you get top dollar for the business you worked so hard to build.

I hope you found the information in this book helpful and that it will serve as a guide to help you make smart financial decisions for your business. I encourage you to reach out and contact me with any questions you may have whether it be about grant writing, Train the Trainer questions, CDA certification, or anything else that I talked about in this book. It is my desire to help every single child care owner better their business and attain the financial freedom and personal success that they desire from owning and operating a child care business.

Lisa Pennington
Daycare Consultant
Childcare Credentialing and Consulting LLC
profitablechildcare@gmail.com
www.startmychildcarebusiness.com

ABOUT THE AUTHOR

Lisa Pennington is a daycare consultant recognized by the Texas Trainer Registry as well as a Texas commercial real estate agent and daycare business broker. Since 2009, Lisa has been assisting child care operators obtain their administrator credentials and regularly assists these providers with all aspects of running a financially successful child care business. From policies and procedures, continued education, and emergency preparedness plans to parent handbooks, Lisa knows what steps need to be taken to make a child care center work in a competitive playing field. She helps hundreds of child care providers every year stay current with state minimums, First Aid training, CPR, and Director Credentialing.

RESOURCES

The following resources were up to date as of the publication of this book. The author is not responsible for changes that have been made following publication. Please research each of the resources independently for the best outcome.

"4 Steps to Creating a Stellar Business Plan." Investopedia. William Artzberger. 01 May. 2008. < http://www.investopedia.com/articles/pf/08/create-business-plan-how-to.asp>

"Can a 501(c)(3) Make a Profit?" Legal Zoom. Wayne Thomas, Demand Media. n.d.
<http://info.legalzoom.com/can-501c3-make-profit-26188.html>

"Can I Set Up An LLC To Avoid Personal Liability In A Lawsuit?" Litigation and Trial. Max Kennerly. 26 May. 2009.
<http://www.litigationandtrial.com/2009/05/articles/att

orney/automobile-accidents/can-i-set-up-an-llc-to-avoid-personal-liability-in-a-lawsuit/>

CDA Competency Standards. Counsel for Professional Recognition. <http://www.cdacouncil.org/the-cda-credential/about-the-cda/cda-competency-standards>

Child Care Compensation. <http://www.daycare.com/news/compensation.html>

Childcare Credentialing and Consulting LLC. <http://www.startmychildcarebusiness.com/director_certificate>

Council for Professional Recognition. <http://www.cdacouncil.org/>

Dental Plans.com <http://www.dentalplans.com>

Exemption Requirements - 501(c)(3) Organizations. Internal Revenue Service. <http://www.irs.gov/Charities-&-Non-Profits/Charitable-Organizations/Exemption-Requirements-Section-501(c)(3)-Organizations>

"Find Business Licenses and Permits." U.S. Small Business Association. n.d. <https://www.sba.gov/licenses-and-permits>

" Limited Liability Company." U.S. Small Business Association. n.d.
<https://www.sba.gov/content/limited-liability-company-llc>

"LLC Advantages for a Home Daycare." Chron. Marina Martin, Demand Media, n.d. Web
<http://smallbusiness.chron.com/llc-advantages-home-day-care-3782.html>

"LLC Basics." Entrepreneur. 31 May. 2005.
<http://www.entrepreneur.com/article/77966>

Minute Menu.
<http://www.minutemenu.com/web/mmkids_features.html>

New Child Care Trainer Requirements. Texas Department of Family Protective Services.
<http://www.dfps.state.tx.us/Child_Care/Day_Care_Licensing/2012-01-31_new_trainer.asp>

The Office of Head Start.
<http://www.acf.hhs.gov/programs/ohs>

Revised Educational Qualifications for the Texas Trainer Registry
<https://tecpds.org/Resource/pdf/trainerregistry/EducationalQualificationsforTTR.pdf>

"Single-Member LLCs and Asset Protection: A 50-State Guide." NOLO Law for All. n.d.
<http://www.nolo.com/legal-encyclopedia/single-member-llcs.html>

"Women-Owned Small Businesses." U.S. Small Business Association. n.d.
<https://www.sba.gov/content/women-owned-small-business-program>

QuickBooks Intuit. <http://quickbooks.intuit.com/>

www.ingramcontent.com/pod-product-compliance
Lightning Source LLC
Chambersburg PA
CBHW030841180526
45163CB00004B/1412